Discovering Science

How Animals Behave

Keith Porter

Facts On File Publications
New York, New York ● Oxford, England

D1377594

Contents

NOTE TO THE READER: while you are reading this book you will notice that certain words appear in **bold type**. This is to indicate a word listed in the Glossary on page 45. This glossary gives brief explanations of words which may be new to you.

Photographic credits

t = top   b = bottom   l = left   r = right   c = center

5 Ferrero Agence Nature/NHPA; 8 John Shaw/NHPA; 9 Anthony Bannister/NHPA; 12 Jany Sauvanet/NHPA; 13 A.P. Barnes/NHPA; 14*t* John Lythgoe/Seaphot; 14*b* Stephen Dalton/NHPA; 15 Anthony Bannister/NHPA; 16/17 Stephen Dalton/NHPA; 18/19 ZEFA; 20 Stephen Dalton/NHPA; 21*t* Peter Scoones/Seaphot; 21*b* Stephen Dalton/NHPA; 22 Richard Beales/Seaphot; 24 Richard Matthews/Seaphot; 25 Dave Currey/NHPA; 28 Ivor Edmunds/Seaphot; 29 Frank Lane Picture Library; 30 Jonathan Scott/Seaphot; 32 K. Ammann/Seaphot; 33*t* Jonathan Scott/Seaphot; 33*b* John Shaw/NHPA; 34 Phillipa Scott/NHPA; 35*t* Anthony Bannister/NHPA; 35*b* Dick Clarke/Seaphot; 36 Roger Tidman/NHPA; 38 Brian & Cherry Alexander; 39 S. & O. Matthews/NHPA; 41 Camilla Jessel; 42 Jeremy Cherfas; 43*t*, 43*b*, 44 World Wildlife Fund

Illustrations by David Anstey

Discovering Science/How Animals Behave

Copyright © BLA Publishing Limited 1987

First published in the United States of America by Facts on File, Inc. 460 Park Avenue South, New York, New York 10016.

All rights reserved. No part of this book may be reproduced or utilized in any form or by any means, electronic or mechanical, including photocopying, recording or by any information storage and retrieval systems, without permission in writing from the Publisher.

Library of Congress Catalog Card Number:
87-80094

Designed and produced by BLA Publishing Limited, East Grinstead, Sussex, England.

A member of the **Ling Kee Group**
LONDON · HONG KONG · TAIPEI · SINGAPORE · NEW YORK

Printed in Italy by New Interlitho

10 9 8 7 6 5 4 3 2 1

The living world

The world is full of living things. The land is covered by green plants. The sea is bursting with life. Birds, bats and insects fly through the air. Even the soil is full of life. All living things have some things in common. They all need air, food and water. They all grow and breed to produce young. All living things also differ from each other. Why should there be so many different types?

Animal surroundings

Each type of plant and animal is suited to certain surroundings, or **environments**. An animal's surroundings affect the way in which it lives. Fish, for example, are suited to life in water. Some types of fish can live only in fresh water. Others survive only in the sea.

The Earth has a great range of environments, from the icy polar regions to the hot deserts. Each environment has its own types of plants and animals.

Changing surroundings

Some environments change with the **seasons**. In cool lands, there are cold winters and warm summers. In hot lands, there are dry seasons and wet seasons. The changing seasons affect the lives of plants and animals. For example, birds nest in the spring. At the end of the summer some of them fly away to warmer lands for the winter.

If we want to study animals, we should know about their surroundings. This helps us to see why they behave in the ways they do.

▲ These ibex are able to live on very steep rocky slopes because their feet give them a good grip.

5

Sunshine and life

All animals need **energy** to move and grow. Animals get energy from the food they eat. Plants also need energy to grow. Unlike animals, plants make their own food.

How plants make food

Plants need energy to make food. The energy they need comes from sunlight. The sunlight is trapped by the plants' leaves. It is used to make sugars. Plants 'mix' sugars with other things to make the food they need. The food can be stored until it is needed.

The Sun's energy is passed through all living things. First, the plants trap energy from sunlight. Then animals eat the plants and so take the stored energy into their bodies. Then, meat-eating animals eat the plant-eaters. The meat-eaters get their energy from the meat.

This movement of energy shows that plants are important to all life. Even meat-eating animals depend on plants. Without the plants, there would be no life on Earth.

peccary

gila monster

jack rabbit

roadrunner

gopher snake

▲ The plants and animals shown here are all used to living in the desert.

butterfly

butterfly

toucan

tree frog

humming bird

macaw

cock of the rock

jaguar

Hercules beetle

armadillo

From deserts to forests

There are many types of environment in the world. They include the deserts, the mountains, the open plains and the forests. Each has its own types of plants. But plants do not grow in all places.

If plants lack warmth or water, they will not grow. The coldest and hottest lands have few plants. Those plants that do live in such harsh places have found special ways to live. Some desert plants have large spongy leaves. These store water. Plants living in the coldest regions have a type of anti-freeze to stop them from freezing.

Only a few animals can live in the hottest and coldest parts of the world. There are too few plants to feed them.

The places with the most plants are the hot, wet parts of the world. These regions are covered with thick jungle, or **rain forest**. The great range of plants means there is a variety of plant food for the animals to live on. It also means that many types of animal can survive. Each is used to certain types of plants. This large range of plant-eaters are **prey** for a large number of meat-eaters.

◀ Energy from the Sun passes through all living things, beginning with plants. The plants are eaten by plant-eaters, like the zebra. Meat-eating animals, such as the lion, then eat the plant-eaters.

▶ The rain forest is one of the richest environments. Most of the animals live in the trees.

7

Flowers and insects

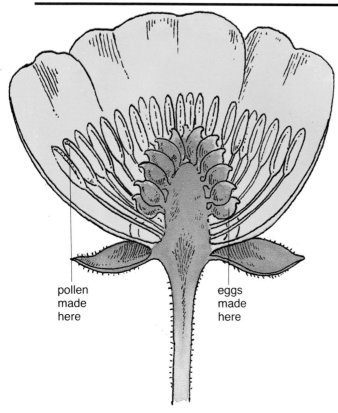

pollen made here

eggs made here

▲ The different parts of a flower.

We have seen that life on Earth could not survive without the plants. In turn, many types of plant need help from animals. This is because of the ways in which these plants **reproduce**.

Why plants have flowers

A few plants, like ferns and mushrooms, grow from tiny specks called **spores**. They need no help from animals. Many plants grow from seeds. To make seeds, a plant produces eggs and **pollen**. These are made in flowers. The 'egg' is kept in a special part of the flower. The pollen is like a fine 'dust'. To make a seed, a grain of pollen has to meet with an egg. This is called **pollination**.

Some pollen is blown through the air by the wind. Plants like grass are pollinated in this way. Many kinds of flower need animals to carry the pollen. Insects are the most important of these animals. A few flowers are pollinated by birds or bats.

Nectar and scent

Flowers have changed shape and color over millions of years. Each plant tries to attract a certain type of insect. One way to do this is to provide food for the animal. Most flowers use **nectar** to

▼ Honey bees fly from flower to flower collecting pollen as food for their young. The pollen sticks easily to their hairy coats.

▲ A hawkmoth uses its long 'tongue' to reach the nectar of this flower.

attract animals. This is a sweet, sugary liquid. It is full of energy.

Insects learn to spot flowers by their color. Each color is a signal. Different colors attract different insects. Bees like yellow, red or purple flowers. Moths like white flowers.

Some flowers use another way of attracting insects. They produce a strong scent. Not all flowers smell pleasant. Some flowers are pollinated by flies. These flowers smell of rotting meat! The flies like the smell.

Insect helpers

Insects that feed on flowers pick up pollen as they feed. The pollen sticks to their bodies. Insects such as beetles pick up less pollen than others. Bees, for example, are well shaped for pollination. Their hairy bodies get covered with pollen as they move from flower to flower. The insects and flowers work together. The plants provide food for the insects. The insects act as a delivery service as they go from plant to plant. Many other animals depend upon the plants which are pollinated by insects.

Trees and animals

Life in a northern pine forest.

Trees are the largest types of plant. They live for a very long time. The oldest known living thing is a tree called the bristle-cone pine. It is more than 4500 years old. Think how many animals must have found shelter in such an old tree!

Food and shelter

Each part of a tree is food for some types of animal. Tiny insects burrow into the leaves and trunk. Larger insects, such as caterpillars, eat the leaves. Birds like to eat fruits, nuts and berries. Larger animals, like monkeys, eat leaves, twigs and fruit. Even the largest land animal, the elephant, is a tree-eater.

Animals do not use trees only for food. Tree branches make good places to build

1. deer 2. black bear 3. hairy woodpecker 4. great gray owl 5. red squirrel

nests. Birds nest in trees to keep their eggs safe. Few ground animals are able to reach birds' nests. Many other animals nest in trees. They are safe resting places.

Trees around the world

Like all plants, each type of tree grows best in certain places. The animals which feed and live on a tree must be used to the same conditions as the tree.

A forest is made of trees and other plants which all like the same conditions.

6. evening grosbeak 7. blue grouse 8. female red crossbill 9. male red crossbill.

There are many types of forests around the world. Each is home to certain types of animals. Let us look at the northern pine forests as an example. Pine forests stretch across the northern parts of North America, Europe and Russia. In these forests, both the trees and animals have many problems to deal with. There are very cold winters and short summers. The ground is frozen for much of the year. Most plants could not survive in such conditions.

Pine trees can survive the bitter cold. They have tough leaves, like green needles. They hold in water, which escapes easily from other types of leaf. This stops the trees from drying out when the ground is frozen.

Pine trees provide little food for animals. Pine needles are not good to eat. Pine trees do not grow flowers or fruit. They have woody **cones** instead. A few animals have **adapted** to feeding on pine trees in the cold north. They include two birds, the blue grouse and the crossbill. The blue grouse is able to eat the pine needles, so it has plenty of food. The crossbill has plenty of food also. It has a special beak which can break open a cone. Cones contain the seeds of the tree. The seeds are good birdfood, but most birds cannot get at them.

Color in animals

Do any colors have their own meanings to you? Think of red and green. Which means stop and which means go? We use these colors as a type of language. Animals also use color as a language.

Yellow and black for danger

Animals with bright colors are often dangerous. Wasps have black and yellow stripes. This is a clear warning that they sting. There are hundreds of stinging insects with this pattern. All animals know that black and yellow stripes are a warning to stay clear.

Some snakes are brightly colored. Coral snakes have bands of red, black and yellow. These colors act as a danger signal. They warn birds to stay away.

▲ Arrow-poison frogs are found in South America. They are some of the most poisonous animals in the world. Indians use the poison on their arrows.

Some animals are poisonous to eat. Any animal which eats them will be ill or may die. Fire-bellied toads and arrow frogs are poisonous to eat. Their red, yellow and black patterns warn of their poisons. Many orange and black butterflies are protected by poisons. Wise animals learn to avoid these creatures.

Some arrow poison frogs contain enough poison to kill 2000 people.

Finding a mate

Birds, butterflies and fish often have bright colors and patterns. The males and females of most of these animals have different colors. Male peacocks, for example, have brilliant colors while the female peahens are dull in color. All these animals can see colors, so they can tell their own kind from others. The patterns also help males to spot females.

Butterflies keep the same patterns for all their short lives. Some types of fish and bird change color as the breeding season comes near. This is to help them attract a mate. For the rest of the year they are dull in color.

It can be dangerous to have bright colors. The colors make an animal easy to see. Their enemies can find them and eat them. This is why female birds are often dull to look at. They have to lay eggs and raise their young. It is better if they are not seen on their nests.

The male animals usually have bright colors. They use their patterns to attract a mate. Male fish, such as some types of tropical fish, often use their patterns as a warning to other males. Each male protects its living space from other males. His color patterns help him to scare off intruders. Other fish know this pattern and go away without a fight.

▼ Can you see this nightjar on her nest? Why do you think her body is such a dull color? Which way is she facing?

How insects see and feel

The world of some animals is very different from ours. Insects are the largest group of animals. They are very different from us. Most of them are only a few centimeters long. They see, smell and feel in different ways.

How insects see

Insects can have two types of eyes. Some insects have both types. One type, called a **simple eye**, is shaped like a tiny bead. It can only tell light from dark. It does not see shapes. Young insects like caterpillars have simple eyes.

The second type of eye is the **compound eye**. Most adult insects have two compound eyes. They are much larger than simple eyes. Each compound eye is made up of thousands of little parts. Each part sees a tiny piece of the whole picture. Insects cannot **focus** like we do. They see only a fuzzy pattern of light, dark and color. Their eyes are best at seeing movement.

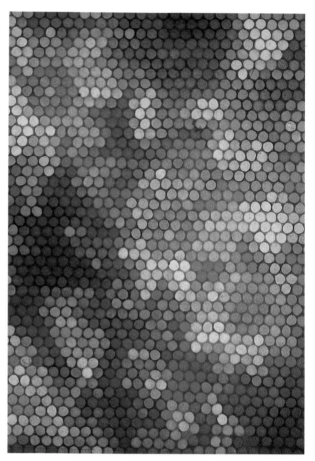

▲ Hold the book away from you. You will see flowers as a bee might see them.

▼ The compound eyes of the horsefly.

Most insects see in color. However, they so not see the same colors as we do. They also see a color of light called **ultraviolet**, which our eyes cannot see. We can tell this by watching a bee in a flower garden. Some of the flowers attract the bee more than others. These flowers have ultraviolet patterns on them. They guide the bee to the middle of the flower, where the nectar is. We can only see these patterns if we use a special camera.

Hairs and feelers

Humans learn about the outside world through the five **senses**. We listen with our ears, taste with our tongue, see with our eyes, smell with our nose. We also feel. Insect senses differ from ours. They can taste and feel with many parts of their body. Most insects can taste food with their feet! Insects also have senses which we do not have. Some can 'see' heat from a long way off. Mosquitoes use this sense to look for warm bodies to bite.

All insects have a pair of feelers, or **antennae**, on their head. These are used as ears, tongues and fingers all in one. Tiny hollows and pits along the antennae pick up smells and tastes.

Some insects use smells to pass on messages. Moths use them to attract a mate. A female luna moth makes a powerful scent. This can attract males from up to five kilometers (11 miles) away. The scent is picked up by the antennae of the male moth.

▼ These feathery antennae of a luna moth are really for 'smelling'. They pick up diffferent scents in the air.

15

Life in the air

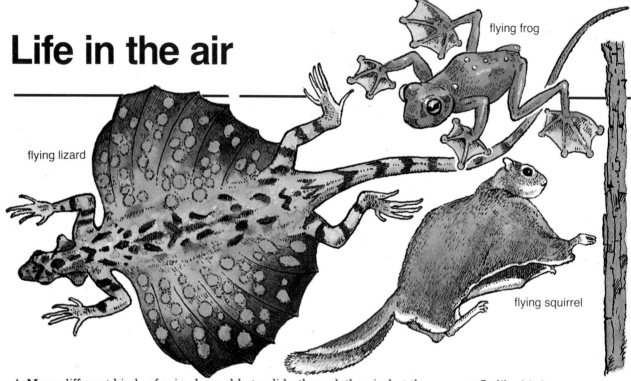

flying frog

flying lizard

flying squirrel

▲ Many different kinds of animal are able to glide through the air, but they cannot fly like birds.

The only true fliers in the animal kingdom are birds, bats and insects. Many so-called flying animals are really gliders. These are the 'flying' snakes, lizards, frogs and squirrels. These animals all climb trees. They simply leap off a branch when they want to reach the ground quickly. They do not have real wings, like birds. Instead, they have flaps of skin which work like tiny parachutes. They slow the animal as it falls to the ground.

There are over 50 types of flying fish. Again, flying fish are not true fliers. A flying fish 'flies' by swimming very fast and then leaping out of the water. It has fins which open up like wings. Some flying fish can glide for 100 m (164 ft).

Flying insects

Insects were the first animals to fly in the air. Flying insects are small and light, but very strong for their size. Some can fly at speeds up to 70 kph (40 mph).

Most insects have two pairs of wings. The flies have only one pair. They are among the best fliers. Dragonflies are excellent fliers. They can hover and even fly backwards.

Insects have strong muscles which are fixed to each wing. The muscles make the wings flap up and down. Each beat

▲ The shape of a bird's wing helps to keep it in the air when flying. If you look at it from the side it has a curved shape. This gives the bird lift.

of a wing pushes down on the air. Most insects beat their wings very quickly. This makes a buzzing noise.

Birds and bats

Insects are helped through the air by the wind. Larger fliers do not stay in the air so easily. Their bodies have to be as

▼ Can you see how this South American moth uses its wings for flying?

light as possible, but strong. Birds have very light bodies for their size. Their feathers weigh very little and many of their bones are hollow. They also have **air sacs** in their bodies. These are small 'balloons' of air. They help the birds to breathe and stay light.

Birds have strong muscles to beat their wings. Once in the air, the shape of a bird's wing helps to keep it in the air. From the side, a bird's wing looks curved. This shape is like an airplane's wing. It helps to give the bird **lift**.

Bats are not related to birds. Bats are the only mammals that can fly. They have very light bodies. Their wings are made of thin skin, stretched over a frame of bones. Bats fly at night, when most birds are asleep. They hunt for insects and other small animals. Some bats fly at up to 50 kph (30 mph). The fastest bird reaches over 150 kph (93 mph)!

Animals that harm us

▲ A sting from this scorpion would be very painful.

▶ This swarm of locusts in Ethiopia covered an area of over 600 square miles.

Most animals do no harm to us, but there are some insects that eat our crops or spread disease. We call these **pests**. There are also other types of animal that can harm or kill people with bites or stings. These include snakes, scorpions and spiders.

Deadly insects

There are a few types of insects that spread disease. They do this by the way they feed. They suck the blood from a sick animal or person. Then they pass the disease on. In tropical countries, one type of female mosquito feeds on human blood. It carries a disease called **malaria**. At one time, millions of people died each year from this disease. People can now take pills which protect them from it.

In parts of Africa, the tsetse fly passes on a disease called sleeping sickness. People can be protected from the disease, but not cattle. The disease kills thousands of cattle. Scientists are trying to find ways of killing off these pests.

Pests that damage crops

Locusts are like large grasshoppers. In parts of Africa, millions of these insects can gather in a huge swarm. The swarm

is blown by the wind. The locusts settle on land where crops grow. In a short time they strip the crops bare. Farmers do not know when a swarm may descend on their land and ruin their crops.

Poisonous animals

Many types of snakes use poison, or **venom**, to kill their prey. They have sharp teeth, called **fangs**. As they bite, the venom goes through the teeth into the victim's flesh.

Snakes also use their teeth to defend themselves. When they are surprised or

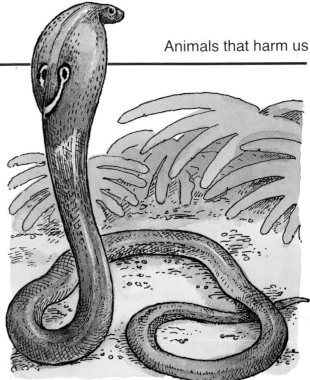

▲ This Indian cobra is one of the most poisonous snakes in the world.

disturbed they move very quickly. They seldom attack people except in self-defense. You should never go near a snake, even if you know that it is a harmless type.

There are several types of snake that are deadly. These are most common in countries where it is hot all the time. They include the Australian tiger snake, the black mamba from Africa and the Indian cobra. The black mamba can move at 11 kph (7 mph), which is about as fast as you can run. Some snakes that are poisonous live in cold countries also. You should beware of all snakes, wherever you live.

A large swarm of locusts may contain 40,000 million locusts.

Social insects

Some insects live together in very large groups. They are called **social insects**. The largest groups are made by bees and ants. A single nest may contain thousands of these insects. It is a 'city' of small animals that like to live together. They have their own strict rules. They keep to a pattern of life which differs from that of other animals.

Working together

The bees that visit flowers are called honeybees. They often make their nests in hollow trees. Some people, called beekeepers, 'farm' bees for their honey. They collect the swarms of bees and put them in wooden boxes called **hives**.

In each hive, there is a single queen bee, larger than the other bees. She spends her life laying eggs. These hatch out as young bees called grubs. As well as the queen, there are several hundred males called **drones**. There are thousands of **worker** bees.

The workers are busy all the time. They divide up the work between them. Some fly out in search of food. They bring back pollen from the flowers and turn it into honey for food. Other workers look after the grubs and keep the nest tidy. They all know what their jobs are.

▼ In the center of this picture is a queen honey bee laying her eggs. Can you tell the difference between the queen and the other bees?

Termites build very large nests. Some termite nests contain several million insects. Termites eat wood and can cause great damage to buildings. The queen termite is much larger than the workers. Some small workers spend their time searching for food. Others are vicious soldiers. A few of these have long snouts which can spray a sticky liquid. These soldiers chase enemies away from the nest.

Insect farmers

Ants and termites often grow their own food. Leaf-cutter ants take pieces of leaves back to their nests. They use the leaves to feed a tiny plant called a **fungus**. This grows on the cut leaves. Then the fungus is collected and eaten by the ants. Some termites also eat fungus. They grow their food in gardens inside the nest. The termites chew up wood and grass before feeding it to the fungus.

▲ It is hard to realize that insects as small as termites have built this huge mound as a home for their colony. There may be as many as two million termites living in the mound.

Ants and termites

Ants usually make their nests under the ground. Each nest is like a very busy city. There are main roads and special chambers. The queen ant lives in her own part of the nest. Here she is looked after by many workers. Some types of ants have workers called soldiers. They are bigger than the other workers and have large jaws. They defend the nest against enemies.

▼ These leaf-cutter ants of South America are carrying leaves to their nest.

Builders and trappers

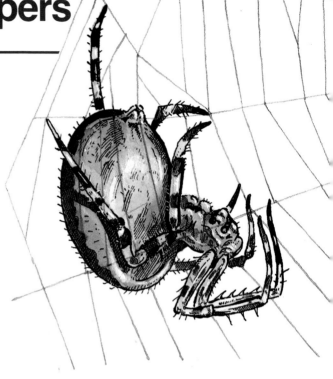

We are not the only animals that are good at building. Many other animals build their own homes. Some build traps to catch their food. The best builders and trappers include spiders, insects and other small animals. Most of them use a kind of glue or thread that comes out of their bodies.

Underwater builders

Corals are tiny animals that live in warm, shallow seas. They grow chalky tubes around themselves. When they die, this hard coral remains. More live corals grow over the dead coral. Year after year, great mounds of coral build up. These become coral reefs and small islands.

▼ Fan worms breathe and feed through feathery tentacles. They live on the sea floor in tubes which they build with grains of sand.

The sea bed is often full of mud or sand. Here fan worms build simple tubes with grains of sand. Some worms glue tubes together side by side. All these tubes are tiny homes where they are safe from enemies.

A spider's web

Spiders feed on flies and other small insects. They are not insects, since they have eight legs. Spiders make a fine thread, called **silk**, which comes out of their bodies. Some spiders use this thread to make a web for trapping their prey.

Spiders' webs are often coated with a kind of glue. Flies are trapped by the glue and cannot escape. Then some spiders wrap up their prey in silk. They make sure that the fly cannot escape or fight back. A spider's web is a beautiful thing, but it is a deadly trap for a fly.

Not all spiders build webs to trap their prey. Some stalk their prey and then

Houses of silk

Insects use silk in other ways. The pure silk that we use for clothes is made by the Chinese silk worm. This is the caterpillar stage of the silk moth. When the caterpillar is fully grown it starts spinning. In about five days it spins a great length of fine silk around itself. This house of silk is called a **cocoon**. Inside the cocoon is the pupa of the silk moth. The cocoons are used in China and Japan to make pure silk for clothing.

Some caterpillars use silk to make leafy tents as safe homes. They use the silk to fasten the edges of the leaves. You may see these in hedges and bushes.

pounce on them. Some can 'spit' out a line of silk to catch an insect. Others use long lines of silk as trip wires.

▼ Silk worms spin cocoons of silk. A cocoon is made up of over 800 yards of silk thread.

Birds and their habits

A bird will fly away as soon as you get too close. It is often not easy to tell what type of bird it is. Birdwatchers use field glasses so that they can watch birds from a distance. This way they can study a group of birds for hours on end. They can learn how each type of bird behaves.

Song and dance

All animals need a space to live in. This space is called a **territory**. Within this space each pair of birds will live and breed. Most birds have small territories. A pair of robins may need only a garden with a few trees in it. They can find enough food there. Some large birds have to go further for their food. The condor of South America has a huge territory. Food is scarce in the Andes mountains where it lives.

All birds need to protect their territories. Birds that live in forests are not easy to see among the trees. They use songs to tell other birds where they live. Each type of bird has its own song.

Sea birds often nest close together in open spaces. They dance about as a way of warning other birds to keep away from their nests.

Choosing a mate

Before breeding, a male bird may mark out an area by singing or dancing. He then has to attract a mate. The male may use song for this. The tune may be different from the one used to protect the home. The female birds choose the best singers to mate with.

▼ Gannets make nesting colonies on cliff tops. Each bird nests just out of pecking range of its neighbors.

▲ A male bird of paradise shows off to his mate.

Birds often use dances to attract a mate. Birds of paradise have fine feathers. The male birds gather together and dance in front of the female birds. They show off their fine feathers. Each female chooses a mate that dances well.

Long journeys

After breeding, many types of bird fly great distances. As winter draws near, swallows fly south from northern Europe. They go to Africa where there will be more food. They stay there until the spring. Then they fly north to breed again. This is called **migration**.

The swallows return to the same building or nesting site where they were hatched. Other types of migrating birds return to the same breeding grounds.

We do not know for certain how birds migrate without losing their way. They may use the Sun by day or the stars by night to help them. They may follow the shape of the land beneath them. Few other animals can find their way so well. We need maps and road signs to help us.

▼ Swallows migrate in large numbers.

Nests and dens

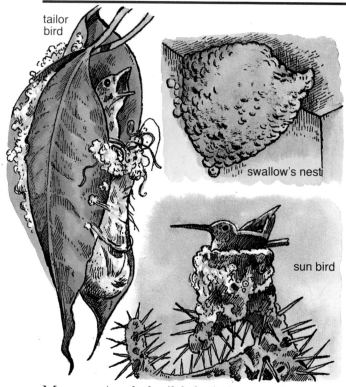

tailor bird

swallow's nest

sun bird

Many animals build their homes for themselves and their families. Nests, dens and burrows are places where animals can keep safe and warm. Here they can hide from their enemies and breed their young.

Birds build their nests and moles build their burrows by **instinct**. Each type of animal makes its own type of home. They go on doing this year after year. They make their homes the same way. They use the same kinds of materials.

Birds' nests

There are thousands of types of birds. Each type makes a different sort of nest. when a pair of birds is ready to breed the male bird chooses a place to make a nest. All nests must be large enough to take the female bird and her brood.

A few types of birds just makes **scrapes** in the ground where the eggs can be laid. Most birds build their nests with greater care. They use grass, twigs and mud. They shape their nests like a cup, so that the eggs cannot roll out. Some birds line the inside of the nest with soft feathers or moss. Other birds build their nests with a hole in the side. Some nest in holes in trees.

Homes under the ground

Small animals often tunnel under the ground to make burrows. Rabbits live in large groups. They join their tunnels to make a **warren**. The rabbits all share the main tunnels. The mothers breed their young in the side tunnels, which are dead ends. The warren is a network of tunnels and homes. Several hundred rabbits may live in one warren.

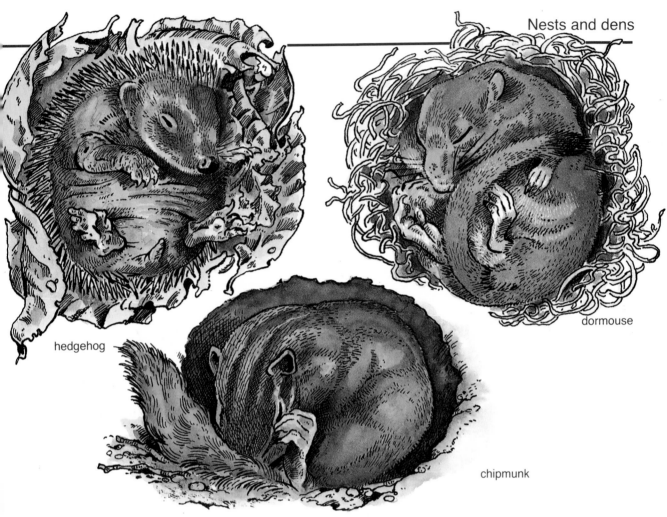

hedgehog

dormouse

chipmunk

Moles live most of their lives in darkness under the ground. They choose soft soil for their long tunnels. Their front legs are well shaped to dig the soil and shovel it aside.

One mole can dig as much as 20 meters (66 ft) of tunnel in one day. As they dig, worms fall down from the roofs of the tunnels. Moles feed on worms and other small animals.

Dens and hiding places

Animals in cold countries often sleep, or **hibernate**, during the cold winter.

Hedgehogs crawl into a heap of dry leaves. Other animals, like bears, dormice and chipmunks live through the winter in dens. Chipmunks store food in their dens. They wake up every few weeks to have a meal. Dormice and bears store their food as body fat.

Animals that hibernate have their own ways of staying alive. Some slow down their breathing. Their hearts beat more slowly, so they use less energy. Others lower their body heat. This lets them use less energy to keep warm. Their winter dens keep them warm and safe from their enemies.

Animal families

▲ A herd of red deer with the stag in the center.
How many females can you count?

What makes animals behave the way they do? All animals need to find food. If their kind is to survive, they must produce young. Feeding amd mating greatly affect the ways in which animals behave.

Family groups

Most types of animals have a male and female form. Some of the simplest animals, like snails, are both male and female at the same time.

The males and females of animals such as birds and mammals each have their own job to do. The females rear the young. They look after them while they grow. The males defend the family group from attack. They have to protect the space in which the family group lives.

Family groups can be made up in many ways. Most bird families have one male, one female and their young. Most mammal families, such as baboons and deer, have one male and several females.

Some animals spend most of their lives alone. They look after themselves as soon as they are born. Such animals do not live in family groups.

Safety in numbers

Animals of the same type often join up into large groups for safety. A lone animal may not see a **predator** sneaking up. A group has many watchful eyes. They all look out for danger.

A group stands a better chance of seeing an attacker. Musk oxen have a clever defense. A young musk ox can easily be killed by wolves. If a pack of wolves comes near a herd of musk oxen, the oxen form a circle, with their horns facing outwards. The hungry wolves cannot get past the horns.

Ape families

The apes are our nearest relatives in the animal kingdom. This makes them interesting to study. Ape families can be very complicated.

Chimpanzees form groups of between 15 and 120. Each group has its own area of land. The females and young stay together. The males are led by a 'boss' male. He keeps order and chases off males from other groups.

▼ Chimpanzees are African apes. They live in groups. A male chimp is being groomed by another one.

Growing and learning

Most young animals need looking after. Rabbits are born blind and helpless. Young birds cannot fly. They need to be fed, protected and taught how to survive. This is the job of their parents.

Caring for the young

Animals with eggs or young can be dangerous. They are best left alone. Swans will attack anything that comes near their nest. Small nesting birds will attack owls and hawks. A bear with her cubs is very dangerous.

Some animals have unusual ways of protecting their young. For example, some parent birds pretend to have a broken wing. This makes an attacker think the bird is an easy kill. Then the parent bird leads the attacker away.

Learning to feed

Young animals learn much from their parents. The parents teach the young how to look after themselves and catch food. The young must also know how to behave with others. Each young animal must know its place in a group.

Many young animals learn by watching their parents. Chicks follow their mother, pecking at anything she pecks at. They soon learn what they can eat. Wolf and lion cubs learn from each other. When cubs are at play, they are learning how to hunt. They learn to creep up and pounce on their brothers and sisters. Lion cubs take a long time to learn how to hunt. Some stay with their mother until they are two years old. By then they will have learned their hunting skills.

▼ This lioness will teach her cubs to hunt for food as they grow up.

▲ A troop of baboons on the move. They live in groups of twenty or more.

Other things are important for survival. Animals must recognize danger. This may come from another animal. It may even come from something like a forest fire. Some of these things are learned as the animal grows, others are known by instinct.

The family grows up

Many animal groups contain one male leader. He often chases away his grown up sons. The young males have to go and make a life for themselves. Some wander alone. Others, like baboons, gather in small bands. The young males may wander for years. When a male is fully grown, it may return to chase off or kill the leader of a group. Then it becomes the new leader.

In some families, the mother also chases away her daughters. They may go to join another group. Some will join a band of wandering males.

Young adult birds have a different life. Most birds find a mate in their second year. Large birds may take three or more years to settle down with a mate. Then they raise a family of their own.

The hunters

Life in the wild is a constant struggle. Animals have to spend much of their lives hunting for food. Many animals, large and small, eat plant foods. These foods are not always in good supply. The animals often have to search far and wide for their food.

Plant-eaters must keep a look-out for predators at all times. Even the life of a predator is not easy. Unlike humans, an animal hunter has no weapons. A tiring chase does not always mean a kill. Without food, a hunter loses strength. This makes the next chase more difficult.

Hunting skills

Each animal hunter has its own way of hunting. Some of the best-known hunters are the large cats. The way they all hunt is affected by the surroundings in which they live. The tiger hunts alone in the forest. It creeps quietly up on its prey, often at night. The cheetah lives in open country. It cannot use surprise to hunt, so instead uses speed.

The cheetah is the fastest land animal over a short distance. It reaches speeds of 100 kph (60 mph). A lot of energy is spent in the cheetah's high-speed dash. It has to make sure of a quick kill, because it cannot keep up a high speed for long.

The lion is a slower animal. It cannot outrun prey such as the wildebeest. The lion uses more cunning than the cheetah. Sometimes, lions hunt in teams. They make a large circle around a group of prey. Then, half of the lions charge at the prey, driving them towards the other lions. The team usually catches one or more wildebeests each time.

▼ An adult giraffe is trying to protect its young from attack by stalking lions.

▲ A group of hunting dogs prepare to attack a herd of wildebeests.

The dog family

Wolves, foxes, jackals, dingoes and the African wild dog all belong to the dog family. These animals are some of the most skilled hunters in the animal kingdom. Some, like foxes, hunt alone. Others hunt in packs. Wolves, jackals and wild dogs often hunt animals much larger than themselves. African wild dogs sometimes hunt zebras. A zebra weighs about eight times as much as a wild dog, and has a very powerful kick. One wild dog would stand little chance of bringing a zebra down. A pack of ten dogs working as a team almost always succeeds.

◀ This osprey has just caught a fish by diving into the water.

Masters of disguise

Animals spend lots of time avoiding predators. Some do this by hiding in their burrows or dens. Many others use color and shape to hide their bodies. This is called **camouflage**. A few animals use camouflage to catch food. They can stay hidden until prey comes near. Then they pounce and catch their prey by surprise.

Color and pattern

All animal patterns have a purpose. When seen in a zoo, the stripes of a tiger seem to stand out. In the jungles of India, the tiger melts into the shadows. The stripes break up the tiger's outline as it walks through the undergrowth.

Most animals are camouflaged for safety. Many birds have speckled feathers which make them very difficult to see on the ground. Lizards, frogs and fish are often camouflaged. Each type has a pattern to match its background. Some lizards have patterns like rock or tree bark. Tree frogs are green to match leaves. Fish have a double camouflage. Their backs are dark to match the sea or river bed. Their bellies are pale colored. From below they are seen against the light sky. Their pale bellies help them match the sky.

▼ The leaf-tailed gecko is a reptile. It can disguise itself to look like the branch of the tree. Can you spot its eye?

Leaves, twigs and flowers

Insects have some of the best disguises. Their bodies can be very strange shapes. Stick insects and stick caterpillars are very good copies of real twigs. Their bodies are long and thin. Some even have bumps, like real twigs. These insects stay very still during the day and search for food at night.

Other insects look like leaves. The Indian leaf butterfly is a perfect copy of a leaf. It even has small blotches and veins, just like a real leaf.

Almost every part of a plant is copied by some insect. There are bugs which look like spines. Others copy the shape and color of flowers or seeds. Nothing is quite what is seems in the insect world.

Some insects copy the patterns of other insects, which are dangerous. Black and yellow hoverflies look like wasps. These flies are copy-cats, or **mimics**. They cannot really sting or bite.

▲ Stick insects have bodies shaped like twigs and branches. How many can you see in this picture?

Changing color

Animal camouflage works only in the right place. A green frog on brown soil is easily seen! Some animals can change color to match different surroundings. The chameleon is a well known animal magician. It can change from green to brown very quickly. This helps it to stay hidden on branches or on leaves.

Many sea animals can change color. A fish called a flounder can match any sandy or pebbly background. Squids, octopuses and shrimps can all change color to match their background.

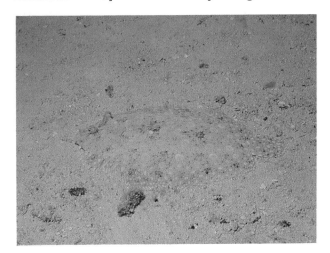

▲ The peacock flounder is hard to see on the sea floor. It has blotches on its back that look like pebbles. Is its head on the right or left of the picture?

Watching animals

▲ Some naturalists build blinds high up among the trees. Here they can watch the forest life for hours.

Even if you live in a city, you can enjoy watching animals. You can watch them in parks and gardens, or when you visit the country. You can watch tame animals in your own home, or in the homes of your friends. It is interesting to learn how animals live their lives. Watch animals carefully. You will soon learn that each type of animal has its own way of behaving. They are all different.

Simple rules

Most animals are timid. They get frightened by sudden movements. Even a tame animal may snap if you put out your hand to stroke it. When you are watching animals you must always keep quiet and still. If you move, you must move slowly.

Some people watch animals for a hobby. They learn to be patient. They try to find a hiding place from which to watch. They use field glasses so that they can watch from a distance. Then they may have to wait for a long time before seeing a rare bird or a small animal.

Rabbits, squirrels and birds all have good eyesight. They will run or fly away if they see you. Remember that rabbits and squirrels will be able to smell you. Try to hide in a place where the wind blows your scent away from the animal.

Looking for signs

In the country, you can sometimes tell that there are animals near by the signs they leave. Large animals, such as deer, leave their footprints in soft ground. Each type of animal has a different footprint. The best time to look at footprints is when there is snow on the ground. Then you can see the marks left by even the smallest animal.

Insects and some small animals often leave signs of their feeding habits. Each type of caterpillar eats the leaves of different plants. Pieces missing out of leaves tell us that caterpillars may be near at hand. If you see empty nut shells on the ground, there may be squirrels or mice nearby. Each type of animal has its favorite food.

Keeping notes

Animal watchers often write down what they see. They also take photographs. It is a good thing to ask yourself questions. Where do woodlice live? What flowers do the bees like best? Where do the swallows build their nests? As you go on watching animals, you will be surprised how much you learn.

Animals that work

Thousands of years ago, our ancestors learned to tame some kinds of wild animal. They found that they could make animals work for them. Oxen were used to pull ploughs and carts. In Asia, people learned how to tame wild horses. They rode on their backs. They used them to draw carts and ploughs. In the Arctic, hunters used reindeer to draw sledges over the snow.

Today, there are still many kinds of animal that work for us. These animals are no longer wild. They do not have to hunt for their food. Instead, they work for their living and are fed by the people who use them.

Animal power

Even today, animals are still used to pull or carry loads. This happens where there are few cars and trucks.

▲ Reindeer are often used to pull sledges in the north of Norway.

▼ For thousands of years oxen have pulled ploughs.

Camels are sometimes used in desert lands to carry heavy loads on their backs. Their wide feet spread the weight of the load and do not sink into the sand. They are adapted to desert life. They can work for days without food or water. In some deserts, heavy trucks are now taking the place of animals.

In the high mountains of South America, there are only steep paths for people to use. Trucks cannot be used here at all. Instead, people use ponies, donkeys and llamas as pack animals. These animals are sure-footed. They can pick their way through large rocks. They can climb steep slopes.

In some parts of the world people still use animals for farm work. In India, small farmers cannot afford to buy tractors. They use oxen to draw ploughs, just as they have always done.

Working dogs

We can also train dogs to work for us. Dogs help us in many ways. They learn quickly, and they have a keen sense of smell. There are many different **breeds** of dog. Each breed of dog is shaped and adapted for one way of life.

The sheepdog is one of the oldest breeds. It was used to protect a herd of sheep from wolves. Now farmers use collies and other sheepdogs to watch the sheep and keep them together.

Some large dogs can be trained to do difficult, but useful jobs. German shepherds are often used as guard dogs and by the police. They use their strong sense of smell to track down criminals. The labrador is a breed that can be trained as a guide dog for blind people. These dogs can help their owners to cross the road in safety.

▼ This shepherd and his dog have to work as a team to keep the sheep together.

Animals in the home

An animal in the home is more than just a friend. All pets have to be fed and cared for. It is the duty of the owner to make sure this is done properly.

Learning about pets

People keep all types of animal as pets. It is important to find out about an animal before owning it. How much exercise does it need? Large dogs need lots of exercise. Is it cruel to keep them in a city? They need plenty of space to run in. How much food, and what food, does a pet need? How large will it grow? Some animals live for many years. Who will care for it in the future?

Some pets come from far off lands. The home they live in will have to suit their needs. Tortoises, for example, are reptiles. They live in the warmer parts

of the world. They must be kept warm.
Their bodies cannot bear too much cold.
Tortoises go into a deep sleep if it is too
cold. Sadly, many tortoises do not get
proper care. This is mainly because the
owners do not understand the animal's
needs. For the winter months, tortoises
should live in a frost-free place. They are
best kept in a box filled with straw while
they are in their deep sleep.

Many pet animals are **social** animals.
They need to be with others of their
kind. We may think that one well-fed
and comfortable rabbit will be happy.
A quick study of rabbits tells us that they
need company. It is much kinder to
keep two or three together.

Animal health

Many pet owners only take their animals
to a **veterinary surgeon**, or vet, when
they are very ill. Some people are put off
because they think the animals will cure
themselves. Others worry about the cost.

The best way to care for an animal is
to prevent illness. Good food, exercise
and clean living conditions are important
to a pet's health. No matter how careful
you are, it is important to keep in touch
with your local vet. Dogs and cats, for
example, can be given injections to
prevent diseases. Vets also advise pet
owners how to look out for illness. A sick
animal cannot tell its owner if it is unwell.
The owner must know all the signs of illness, and what to do if a pet does get sick.

▶ Puppies who visit the vet from an early age
quickly make friends, and get used to surgery visits.

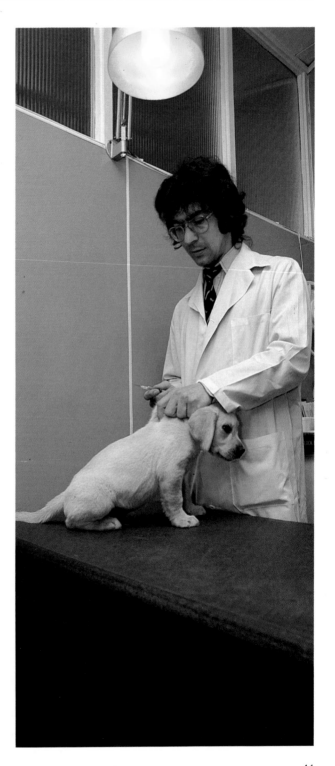

Zoos and wildlife reserves

It is thought that the ancient Egyptians were the first to keep wild animals. They kept giraffes, monkeys and zebras. This was 3000 years ago. About 200 years ago, the first zoos were started in Europe. At that time, each zoo tried to keep as many types of animal as it could. Zoos were like museums. The animals were kept in small cages. They were not well cared for.

Modern zoos

The zoos of today are very different. They are places where animals have the room to move around. Instead of cages, they have **enclosures** for the animals. Each one is made to match the animal's normal surroundings.

At the London zoo there is a large space for birds to fly about in. It also has a special house for night animals. It is called a 'moonlit' house. The lighting is low enough for the animals to come out to feed. They think it is night, though it is day. The Bronx Zoo, in New York, also has a house for night animals.

Each zoo tries to be expert in a few types of animal. This way they can give a better life to the animals. Visitors watch the animals as though in the wild.

Those who run zoos want to help wildlife. Some zoos have been able to breed rare types of animals. Sometimes they return them to the wild.

▼ In modern zoos, like this one in Chicago, animals do not live in small cages. This gorilla lives in an environment very like its natural one.

Wildlife reserves

There is another way to protect rare animals. This is by protecting the places where they live. These places are made into **reserves**. This is land where no one can farm, or hunt or cut down trees.

Giant pandas live in a part of China. They feed only on a plant called bamboo. Reserves have been made for the pandas to try and save them from dying out. From time to time, the bamboo dies back. This means that the pandas have very little food. So people are trying to save this plant, also. It is the only plant that keeps the few pandas alive.

There are wildlife reserves all over the world. Some of these are to protect one type of animal. The Javan rhino is now only found on one reserve in Java. Large reserves in India have been set aside for tigers. Huge areas of Africa and North America are kept as National Parks. In these places, many animals are now safe.

▲ This giant panda has been put to sleep for a few minutes by Chinese scientists. They will measure it to make sure it is getting enough food.

▼ The Javan rhino is one of the rarest animals in the world. This rhino is standing in water to keep cool.

Caring for wildlife

▲ This polar bear has been injured. Scientists have come to its rescue. Later they will return it to the wild.

We share the Earth with countless animals. Each type of animal is used to living in certain surroundings. Human beings have made many changes. Forests have been cleared. Marshes and swamps have been drained. Much land has been taken for farmland. Towns and roads now cover large areas.

As we take more and more of the Earth, there is less space for wildlife. Without a home, wildlife has to move on or die out. In the past, people cleared the land and did not think of wildlife. Animals were hunted, often until there were none left.

About 100 years ago, some people began to form the first animal **conservation** groups. In Britain, one such group called itself the Fur, Fin and Feather Folk. They tried to put a stop to the needless killing of animals. Since that time, many groups have been formed. Their efforts have made many people aware of the harm being done.

One of the best-known groups is the World Wildlife Fund set up in 1961. Since then it has helped in thousands of wildlife projects. Some of the well-known animals it has helped to save are the giant panda, tiger, polar bear and mountain gorilla.

Many people now know that plants, animals and people have to live together. There is still time to stop the destruction.

Glossary

adapt: to change so as to suit changing surroundings and conditions

air sac: an air-filled sac in a bird's body. Air sacs help birds to breathe when they are flying

antenna: one of a pair of long feelers found on the heads of insects

breed: a kind or class of animal

camouflage: the patterns, colors or body shapes which help animals to blend with their surroundings

cocoon: a case of spun threads that a caterpillar or insect larva spins around itself

compound eye: a type of insect eye made up of many parts. Each part sees a tiny portion of the object being viewed

cone: the part of a conifer tree which contains the seeds

conservation: the protection of animals and plants, and their natural surroudings

drone: a male bee which does no work

enclosure: an area of ground surrounded by a fence

energy: the power to do work

environment: all the surroundings and conditions in which animals and plants live

fang: a long, curved tooth. A snake's fangs inject poison into the snake's prey

focus: to produce a sharp, clear image by using a lens

fungus: any one of a large group of simple plants which include yeasts, moulds, rusts and mushrooms

hibernate: to spend the winter in a resting or sleeping state

hive: a special case or box used for keeping bees

instinct: a form of behavior that most animals are born with. Instinct does not have to be learned

lift: the force that keeps a bird in the air, helped by the shape of its wings

malaria: a disease that causes high fever, chills and sweating. It is passed to people by a type of female mosquito which feeds on human blood

migration: a long journey made by an animal at certain times of the year. Animals often migrate to escape harsh winters which lead to shortage of food

mimic: an animal imitator, or copy-cat. Some harmless insects mimic others that sting or bite

nectar: a sweet liquid made inside some types of flower. Insects like to feed on nectar

pest: an animal which eats or destroys things of value, or causes disease

pollen: tiny grains produced by flowering plants. Pollen causes other plants to grow seeds when it is carried to them

pollination: the moving of pollen from one flower to another, so that new seeds can grow. Pollination is usually carried out by the wind, or by insects which pick up pollen on their bodies

predator: any animal that hunts and eats other animals

prey: an animal that is hunted and eaten by another animal

rain forest: a hot, damp type of forest found in areas close to the Equator. Rain forests are thick with trees and plants

reproduce: to produce offspring. Only living things can reproduce

reserve: an area of land in which wildlife can live without threat from people

scrape: a simple type of bird's nest made on the ground

season: one of the main periods in the yearly wether cycle. The four seasons are spring, summer, fall and winter

sense: one of the powers which animals have to make them aware of their surroundings. Humans have five senses: sight, hearing, taste, smell and touch

silk: a fine thread which is produced by a silkworm. Silk is made into thread for sewing and into cloth

simple eye: a simple type of eye found in some insects. Simple eyes can only tell light from dark

social: used to being with others

social insect: one of a group of insects that live together in colonies. Ants, termites and bees are social insects

spore: a tiny cell produced by certain plants. Spores are spread by the wind. They grow into new plants when conditions are suitable

territory: an area of land in which an animal or group of animals live, feed and breed. Animals mark out their territory by scent, or, in the case of birds, by singing

ultraviolet: a part of sunlight invisible to humans

venom: a poison produced by snakes and other types of animal. Venom is injected into a body by a bite or sting

veterinary surgeon: a person who deals with diseases and injuries in animals

warren: a system of rabbit burrows which join up under the ground

worker bee: a type of female bee which does not lay eggs. It is smaller than a queen or drone, and does all the work in a hive, and also flies out to gather food